BETHLEHEM'S
BIG
NIGHT

BETHLEHEM'S BIG NIGHT

*A full-length musical Christmas play
with additional yuletide sketches*

by MARTHA BOLTON

Bethlehem's Big Night
Copyright © 1995 by Martha Bolton. All rights reserved.

Print rights administered by Lillenas Publishing Co.

Production Instructions for the musical play *Bethlehem's Big Night* (pages 13 to 44):

No part of this publication may be reproduced, stored in a retrieval system, or transmitted, in any form or by any means, electronic, mechanical, photocopying, recording, or otherwise, without the prior permission of the copyright administrator.

This is a royalty play. Permission to perform these works is granted when a Production Pack containing scripts for the cast and director is purchased and the royalty is paid two weeks prior to the performance(s). The performance-licensing fee for this musical play is $15.00 for the first performance and $10.00 for each subsequent performance. Please use the form in the back of this book to register your performance(s) and to submit the royalty payment. You may make copies of the form or submit the information in the form of a letter.

The following should appear in your printed program:
"Produced by special arrangements with Lillenas Publishing Company."

Production Instructions for the additional holiday Christmas sketches (pages 45 to 58):

Amateur performance rights and photocopy permission is granted when two copies of this work are purchased. This applies only to sketches and monologues.

Please include the following on each reproduced copy:
From *Bethlehem's Big Night,* copyright © 1995 by Martha Bolton. All rights reserved. Used with permission.

Questions? Please write or call:
Lillenas Publishing Company
P.O. Box 419527
Kansas City, MO 64141
Phone: 816-931-1900 • Fax: 816-412-8390
E-mail: drama@lillenas.com
Web: www.lillenasdrama.com

Printed in the United States.

Cover art by Paul Franitza

Dedication

To Bob and Dolores Hope
. . . for so many years of helping to bring the spirit of Christmas
to our troops at home and abroad

CONTENTS

Acknowledgments 9

Preface 11

Bethlehem's Big Night—script..................................13

Holiday Christmas Sketches
  The Scrooge Patrol 47
  The Sweatshop..50
  Tree Talk..52
  Shopper Stopper. 55
  I Did It All Myself 56

Bethlehem's Big Night—songs...................................59
  Bethlehem's Big Night....................................59
  No One Special 65
  No One Special (reprise) 71
  You're Welcome Here 73
  Right Here in Bethlehem..................................82
  When You Make Room for Him 89
  Jesus, Welcome to Your World 95
  Finale...101

ACKNOWLEDGMENTS

A special thanks to:

My husband, Russ, who never complained about all those nights when I had to rush off to play practice and couldn't cook his dinner. (Come to think of it, he always looked a little relieved!)

My sons, Russ, Matt, and Tony, who have worn so many Bible-time costumes, they're beginning to think that's the style.

Paul Miller, who has become more like a brother than an editor. I appreciate your friendship, your talent, and your enthusiastic support of Christian drama.

And finally, to the performers, directors, stage crew, and all those I had the privilege of working with early in my writing career—thanks for allowing me to learn from you.

PREFACE

In writing and directing numerous Christmas pageants over the years, I've learned some pretty valuable lessons. The main lesson is that no matter what the production looks like at dress rehearsal (and for some reason, that's when whatever can go wrong usually will), don't panic. God always works out those problems, and the performance ends up going more smoothly than you hoped.

Another important tip is to not attempt to do everything yourself. There are people in your congregation who have been given certain gifts and might be waiting for an opportunity to use them. Make an announcement for anyone who can help sew costumes, build sets, do makeup, etc. You might be surprised, not only by those who step forward, but also by the enthusiasm with which they volunteer.

Be sensitive to those performers who are stepping out onstage for the first time. Help it be a positive experience for them. I can't tell you how many times I've seen someone agree to take a bit part in one play (after a good deal of coaxing), then enjoy it so much that they volunteer for a leading role in the next production.

Lastly, don't forget to have a good time. Everyone is under pressure—the director, the actors, the set designer, the wardrobe people, everyone. You have no idea what they're having to go through just to make it to those rehearsals. They have no idea how much work you're doing behind the scenes. So, be serious when you need to be serious, laugh whenever you can laugh, and always remember that the purpose behind the Christmas pageant is to tell the story of how God loves the world so much that He sent His Son, Jesus, to be born in a manger some 2,000 years ago.

If you keep all this in mind, your production can't help but be a success—both onstage and behind the scenes as well.

BETHLEHEM'S BIG NIGHT

MASTER CAST LIST

MARY
JOSEPH
BABY JESUS
REBECCA
ABIGAIL
RACHELLE
NARRATOR
MARTHA
BARTHOLOMEW
RUTH
TRAVELER NO. 1
SILAS

MERCHANT NO. 1
MERCHANT NO. 2
TOWNSPERSON NO. 1
TOWNSPERSON NO. 2
LEAH
SHAMICH
JOSIAH
HEBOAM
TYRUS
ANGEL (voice over P.A. only)
TOWNSPEOPLE
MERCHANTS

MASTER PROP LIST

Four stools or several benches
Large piece of cloth
Needles and thread
Broom
2 "Honey Do" lists, written on
    scrolls—one long, one short
Bucket and rags
4 signs
    2 Vacancy signs, one larger than
        the other
    1 sign that says Only 8 Rooms Left
    1 No Vacancy sign
Marker or writing utensil
Plants and greenery

Rocks, at least one sturdy enough for
    Mary to sit on (can be a stool,
    covered to look like a rock)
Various foods and wares for
    merchants
Buckets and cloths
Ladder
Shepherds' staffs
A stew pot
Bowls
Eating utensils
Manger
Hay
Various items to give the look of a
    stable

SET SUGGESTIONS

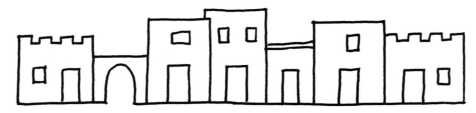

The skyline of Bethlehem should remain central throughout the play.

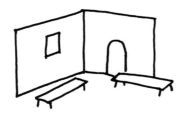

Mary's home would be at stage right.

For later scenes, Mary's home can be converted by folding the flats, turning them around into the Motel Six Shekels.

At stage left, we would have the Bethlehem Inn, which would later be converted into the stable.

All other action would take place center stage.

Opening Scene

(The play opens with the cast [or choir] dressed in Bible-time costumes excitedly singing the following number on the streets of Bethlehem. The skyline of Bethlehem should be in the background.)

Bethlehem's Big Night

(Verse 1)
O Bethlehem, O little town,
How bless'd you are today!
A visitor is coming!
Good news is on the way!

God's chosen you! There's work to do!
His calendar won't wait!
O Bethlehem, rejoice now!
Get set for something great!

(Chorus)
Be-be-be-bethlehem
Ho-ho-ho-holy town,
What's scheduled here will clearly
Turn the world right upside down!
It's time to raise your voice!
Join heav'n and rejoice!
God has some mighty big plans
For you, O Bethlehem!

(Verse 2)
O Bethlehem, O little town,
So humble in your ways.
It's time for you to shine now,
Lift up your voice in praise!

Don't ever think that you're too small
To be thought highly of,
For God looked down and chose you
To show the world His love!

(Chorus)
Be-be-be-bethlehem,
Ho-ho-ho-holy town,
What's scheduled here will clearly
Turn the world right upside down!
It's time to raise your voice!
Join heav'n and rejoice!
God has some mighty big plans
For you, O Bethlehem!
God has some mighty big plans
For you, O Bethlehem!

(NOTE: As cast sings last two lines of the song, they divide and begin exiting the stage while keeping their attention focused on the Bethlehem skyline. The skyline lights slowly fade and we . . .

(Blackout)

SCENE 2

Characters: MARY
REBECCA
ABIGAIL
RACHELLE
JOSEPH

Setting: Mary's home

Props: Four stools or several benches
Large piece of cloth
Needles and thread

Costumes: Bible-time clothing

(When the lights come up, we see MARY *and her friends sitting on the stools, stitching the piece of cloth.* MARY *seems preoccupied.)*

REBECCA: Mary, what's wrong? Your mind seems a million miles away.

RACHELLE: It wouldn't happen to be on someone by the name of Joseph now, would it?

ABIGAIL: If Joseph were *my* boyfriend, my mind would be on him too.

REBECCA: If Joseph were your boyfriend, *his* mind would need examining!

*(*REBECCA *and* RACHELLE *laugh;* ABIGAIL *gives* REBECCA *an insincere smile.)*

ABIGAIL: And just how many men have asked for *your* hand in marriage, Rebecca?

REBECCA: Do you want the exact number, or can I round it off?

ABIGAIL: Round it off.

REBECCA: Very well . . . *(Enthusiastically begins counting it off on her fingers. First, she counts to eight, then four, then . . .)* All right . . . zero. But that doesn't mean they haven't thought about it!

RACHELLE: Just as we figured.

*(*JOSEPH *enters.)*

JOSEPH: Mary, can I speak with you?

(MARY *looks at her friends as if to ask if they'd mind.*)

REBECCA: Go on. *(Indicating cloth)* We can finish this.

(MARY *exits the home with* JOSEPH. *They walk to center stage and mime chatting.*)

RACHELLE: What do you think they're talking about?

ABIGAIL: It's none of our concern. *(Goes to doorway and pretends to listen)* . . . but I sure wish they'd speak up!

REBECCA: Girls, girls . . . let them have their privacy.

ABIGAIL: You're right. You're absolutely right. *(As she walks back to her seat, she leans her head back, trying to sneak in one last listen)*

REBECCA: Abigail!

ABIGAIL: Oh, all right.

(Disappointed, ABIGAIL *sits, and they continue with their sewing. The lights dim on* MARY's *home, and our attention is drawn to* MARY *and* JOSEPH *center stage.*)

JOSEPH: Mary, I've been thinking about what you told me today.

MARY: I don't fully understand it either, Joseph. But you must believe me.

JOSEPH: I believe you, Mary. And I've come to tell you I'll be here for you.

(JOSEPH *and* MARY *sing the song together.*)

No One Special

MARY: I'm no one special.
Why did He choose me?
I'm just one person.
How can He use me?

Why do I matter?
What is His holy plan?
Why would He choose me?
I don't understand.

JOSEPH: Don't second-guess Him,
You're who He chooses.
A willing vessel
Is what He uses.

You're someone special.
He knows what you're to do.
What He is asking,
He will see you through.

MARY: Can't comprehend it—
Why He should need me.

JOSEPH: He has chosen you,

MARY: All I can do is . . .

JOSEPH: He will see you through.

MARY: . . . trust Him to lead me.

BOTH: So much has happened,
So much to think about.

MARY: But I'll always serve Him,
And I'll never doubt.

BOTH: Yes, we'll always serve Him,
and we'll never doubt.

JOSEPH *(after song):* God will be with you, Mary.

MARY: I know Joseph. *(A beat)* You'd better go now.

(JOSEPH *gives* MARY *a slight hug, then exits. As the lights come up on* MARY'S *home, we see* REBECCA *and* RACHELLE *are busy sewing.* ABIGAIL *is at the window, peeking. When she sees* MARY *approaching, she rushes back to her seat.)*

ABIGAIL: She's coming! She's coming! (ABIGAIL *sits just as* MARY *enters the home. Out of breath, but trying not to appear so.)* Is everything all right, Mary?

MARY: I just have a lot on my mind.

ABIGAIL: Well, if you ever need someone to confide in, you can trust me.

(RACHELLE *and* REBECCA *look at* ABIGAIL *like she's the last person on earth anyone would want to confide in.)*

MARY: I appreciate your concern, my friends, but what I'm facing, I must guard in my heart.

REBECCA: Whatever it is, it must be good news. You look radiant!

RACHELLE: You do have a certain glow about you, Mary.

ABIGAIL *(dying of curiosity):* You don't want to give us a little hint?

MARY: I can't.

RACHELLE: Then at least tell us this much . . . is it?

MARY: Is it *what?*

RACHELLE: Good news?

MARY: It's the best news this world has ever or will ever know.

(MARY sings "No One Special" reprise)

MARY: Can't comprehend it—
    Why He should need me.
    All I can do is
    Trust Him to lead me.

    So much has happened,
    So much to think about.
    But I'll always serve Him,
    And I'll never doubt.

(*After song, the girls look at* MARY *with both admiration and curiosity for what her future might hold, and we* . . .

(Blackout)

Scene 3

Characters: JOSEPH
NARRATOR
ANGEL (voice heard over P.A. only)

(A narrow spotlight picks up JOSEPH *resting center stage. He looks up into the light, as though he's seeing an angel.)*

NARRATOR *(offstage):* And an angel of the Lord appeared unto Joseph in a dream, saying . . .

ANGEL: "Joseph, thou son of David, fear not to take unto thee Mary thy wife: for that which is conceived in her is of the Holy Ghost."

(Blackout)

Scene 4

Characters: NARRATOR
MARTHA
BARTHOLOMEW
RUTH
TRAVELER NO. 1

Setting: Bethlehem (*Skyline of Bethlehem is in the background, with an inn on either side of the stage. The inn at stage right is called Motel Six Shekels. The inn at stage left is called Bethlehem Inn [see sketch on page 16].*)

Props: Broom
2 "Honey Do" lists, written on scrolls—one long, one short (BARTHOLOMEW *has the longer one in his pocket;* MARTHA *has the shorter one in her pocket.*)
Bucket and rags
Three signs—2 Vacancy signs,
1 sign that says Only 8 Rooms Left
Marker or writing utensil

Costumes: Bible-time clothes

(*During the following narration, the stage lights slowly come up. It's early morning in Bethlehem. In the background we hear faint music played, perhaps "O Little Town of Bethlehem." There is a vacancy sign posted at the Bethlehem Inn.*)

NARRATOR: "It came to pass in those days, that there went out a decree from Caesar Augustus, that all the world should be taxed. . . . And all went to be taxed, every one into his own city."

(MARTHA *steps out of the Bethlehem Inn door, carrying a broom. She begins sweeping off the porch area, but before long she calls to someone inside . . .*)

MARTHA: Bartholomew! Bartholomew!

BARTHOLOMEW (*sleepily from inside the Bethlehem Inn*): What is it, wife?

MARTHA: Rise up and get out here! We've much work to do!

BARTHOLOMEW (*still unseen by audience*): But this is my day to rest.

MARTHA: *Every* day is your day to rest!

24

BARTHOLOMEW: And this is one of them.

MARTHA: Bethlehem will be swarming with visitors coming to register for Caesar's tax. We want to entice *some* of those travelers to stay with us.

BARTHOLOMEW: We do?

MARTHA *(dusting off the Vacancy sign):* We've got beds to make, meals to prepare . . .

BARTHOLOMEW *(poking head out of window):* . . . naps to take.

MARTHA: Bartholomew! You are the most . . .

(RUTH *steps out of the Motel Six Shekels door carrying two signs. When* MARTHA *sees her standing there, her tone of voice suddenly changes.)*

MARTHA *(lovingly):* . . . wonderful husband I could have ever hoped for.

RUTH: Oh, let him sleep. We'll be happy to accommodate any weary travelers who happen by this way.

(RUTH *hangs up the first sign. It's a much bigger Vacancy sign than* MARTHA*'s.)*

MARTHA: I'm sure you would, dear neighbor. *(Flashes an insincere smile)*

(RUTH *hangs up the second sign, which says Only 8 Rooms Left, then smiles and exits back through the door of her inn.)*

MARTHA: Bartholomew! Why aren't you out here?!

BARTHOLOMEW *(opens the door of the inn and steps out):* When I took thy hand in marriage, why didn't someone warn me that thy mouth went with it?

MARTHA: What's that?

BARTHOLOMEW: I said, "Coming, dear."

MARTHA: Well, it's about time! Now then, I've made a list of things you'll need to do today.

BARTHOLOMEW: *Another* list? What shall I do with the list you gave me last week? *(He takes a scroll out of his pocket and unrolls it. The audience sees it's the longest "Honey Do" list in history.)*

MARTHA: Add this to it. *(She takes another "Honey Do" list from her pocket and hands it to him.)*

BARTHOLOMEW: You'll have me working till the Messiah comes!

MARTHA: Then so be it! We have vacant rooms that must be filled with paying customers. Now, get busy, husband!

BARTHOLOMEW *(under his breath):* Wasn't it King Solomon who said "a continual dripping on a very rainy day and a contentious woman are alike"?

MARTHA: What's that?

BARTHOLOMEW: I said, "I live to please you, dear."

(BARTHOLOMEW *picks up a bucket and a few rags nearby, then exits stage left.* TRAVELER NO. 1 *enters and looks over both motels.* MARTHA *and* RUTH *can hardly contain their excitement.* TRAVELER NO. 1 *cannot decide between the two motels. First, he starts to walk toward Motel Six Shekels, then stops and turns back to the Bethlehem Inn. He stops again and turns back to Motel Six Shekels. Finally, he stops and walks back to the Bethlehem Inn.*)

TRAVELER NO. 1 (*addressing* MARTHA): Do you have a room for the night?

MARTHA (*glancing in* RUTH's *direction and speaking loud enough to make sure* RUTH
 hears): Do I have a room? *Do I have a room?*

(MARTHA *and* RUTH *break into "You're Welcome Here" song. Throughout the following number,* TRAVELER NO. 1 *is pulled between* MARTHA *and* RUTH *at the appropriate moments.*)

You're Welcome Here

MARTHA: You're welcome here! We say "Shalom!"
    Your room awaits; feel right at home!
    We've got clean towels, and we've got ice.

RUTH: . . . And don't forget to mention mice!
    We've got much more to offer you!
    We've got it all . . .

MARTHA: . . . and bedbugs too!
    Come in and rest your weary feet.

RUTH: Stay here instead. We change our sheets!

    (*Chorus*)
BOTH: Do you need a place to stay?
    No reservations? That's OK.

RUTH: For only six shekels per day . . .
    You're welcome *here!*

MARTHA: Staying *here* makes perfect sense.
    For we will treat you like a prince.
    And on your pillow we'll leave mints!

BOTH: You're welcome here!

RUTH: Our wake-up calls are never late.

MARTHA: Their beds feel like a wooden crate!

RUTH: Our rooms are air-conditioned too!

MARTHA: Sure, when the roof caves in on you!
Our swimming pool's the best around.

RUTH: It's just a puddle in the ground!
I cook the meals for all our guests.

MARTHA: . . . That's true, and now in peace they rest!

BOTH: Do you need a place to stay?
No reservations? That's OK.

RUTH: For only six shekels per day.
You're welcome *here!*

MARTHA: Staying *here* makes perfect sense,
For we will treat you like a prince.
And on your pillow, we'll leave mints!

RUTH: You're welcome here!

RUTH *(spoken)*: Did I say *six* shekels per day? I meant *five*. *(She crosses out the "six" on the Motel Six Shekels sign and makes it a five.)*

MARTHA *(pulling* TRAVELER NO. 1 *in her direction): Four* shekels! You won't find a better rate in all of Bethlehem!

RUTH *(crosses out the "five" on her sign and makes it a "three")*: Three shekels and we'll throw in a continental breakfast!

MARTHA: Only *two* shekels for a nice, clean room with a view.

RUTH: A view of *what?* Your *stable?*

MARTHA: A stable's not so bad.

RUTH: That depends on which way the wind is blowing! *(To* TRAVELER NO. 1*)* *One* shekel . . . and valet parking for your donkey.

TRAVELER NO. 1: I'll take it!

*(*RUTH *smiles triumphantly, and as she escorts* TRAVELER NO. 1 *through her inn door, she sings . . .)*

RUTH: You're welcome here! *(Spoken)* Come right on in! (RUTH *and* TRAVELER NO. 1 *exit through Bethlehem Inn door.)*

MARTHA *(crosses her arms and says in a huff)*: That woman's done it once again! *(Calling offstage)* Bartholomew! Bartholomew!

(Blackout)

Scene 5

Characters: NARRATOR
MARY
JOSEPH

Setting: On the road to Bethlehem

Props: Plants and greenery, giving the illusion that this is somewhere on the road to Bethlehem
Rocks, at least one that is sturdy enough for Mary to sit on

Costumes: Bible-time clothing
(Mary is about 9 months pregnant)

(The spotlight finds MARY *and* JOSEPH *center stage. The cluster of plants is behind them. They've just interrupted their journey for a brief rest.)*

NARRATOR: "And Joseph also went up from Galilee, out of the city of Nazareth, into Judaea, unto the city of David, which is called Bethlehem; (because he was of the house and lineage of David:) to be taxed with Mary his espoused wife, being great with child."

MARY: How much farther, Joseph?

JOSEPH: Bethlehem's there . . . *(pointing)* in the distance. We should reach it by nightfall.

MARY *(weakly):* But I'm so weary, Joseph.

JOSEPH: I know. We'll rest here for a moment, then continue.

*(*MARY *sits on a nearby rock. After a brief pause . . .)*

MARY: Joseph . . .

JOSEPH: Yes, Mary?

MARY: What do you think God has planned for this baby?

JOSEPH: The angel said that the babe was to be called "Jesus," and that He would save the people from their sins.

MARY: Yes, but how will that be, Joseph? Only a blood sacrifice can redeem us from sin.

JOSEPH *(there is an uncomfortable pause, realizing what this might mean):* We should continue on our journey. Evening will be here soon.

(JOSEPH *helps* MARY *stand, and as they continue toward Bethlehem, we . . .*

(Blackout)

Scene 6

Characters: BARTHOLOMEW
SILAS
MERCHANT NO. 1
MERCHANT NO. 2
TOWNSPERSON NO. 1
TOWNSPERSON NO. 2
NUMEROUS TOWNSPEOPLE AND MERCHANTS

Setting: Streets of Bethlehem—day

Props: Various foods and wares for merchants
Buckets and cloths
Ladder (should be placed somewhere near the Bethlehem Inn)

Costumes: Bible-time clothing

(Scene opens with the streets of Bethlehem filled with activity. The townspeople are visiting with each other, buying from the street merchants, etc. SILAS is cleaning around Motel Six Shekels. BARTHOLOMEW enters through doorway, bucket and cloths in hand.)

SILAS *(noticing* BARTHOLOMEW*)*: You're up early this morning.

BARTHOLOMEW: When I felt the warmth of the sunlight upon my face this morning, I said to myself, "How can I waste this gorgeous day by merely sleeping it away?" So I quickly dressed and rushed out here to bask in the glory of this moment.

SILAS: Your wife told you to get up and get to work, too, huh?

BARTHOLOMEW: You got it! *(He starts washing down his wall.)* But that's all right. These things do need to get done.

SILAS: Can you believe how crowded Bethlehem is today?

BARTHOLOMEW: I never thought I'd be happy for a new tax, but it sure has helped business.

SILAS *(a beat):* Can I ask you something?

BARTHOLOMEW: I know, I know. You want to borrow the ladder again.

SILAS: No . . .

BARTHOLOMEW: Aw, don't worry about it. It's your turn anyway. Remember, I borrowed it from you last spring. You borrowed it from me last summer. And I borrowed if from you in the fall.

SILAS: By the way, whose is it anyway? It's gone back and forth so many times, I've forgotten.

BARTHOLOMEW: Me too.

MERCHANT NO. 1 *(walks over in a huff):* It's mine!

(He takes the ladder back to his place of business, sets it down, then resumes his selling. SILAS *and* BARTHOLOMEW *look at each other and shrug.)*

SILAS *(to* BARTHOLOMEW*):* What I was about say is there's something—I can't put my finger on it—but there's something in the air . . .

BARTHOLOMEW: All right, all right. Cleaning the stable is next on my list.

SILAS: No. It's not your stable. This is different. It's just a feeling . . . a feeling like something wonderful is about to happen right here in Bethlehem.

BARTHOLOMEW: Some say cleaning out my stable would be wonderful.

SILAS *(continuing, as if he didn't hear him):* It's something so wonderful, we can't even comprehend it!

TOWNSPERSON NO. 1: Excuse me, but I couldn't help overhearing your conversation. I've been having that same feeling too.

SILAS: You have?

(Music should begin playing under the following talk.)

TOWNSPERSON NO. 1: I can't explain it, but it's plainly something great!

TOWNSPERSON NO. 2: Yes, I agree with everything you say!

MERCHANT NO. 1: It's something wonderful!

TOWNSPERSON NO. 1: Perhaps stupendous!

SILAS: It just might be the best news to ever come our way!

*(*SILAS *breaks into song, "Right Here in Bethlehem.")*

Right Here in Bethlehem

(Chorus)

SILAS: It's in our hearts!

TOWNSPERSON NO. 1: It's on the wind!

ALL: Something good is waiting around the bend!

TOWNSPERSON NO. 2: We're on the brink

MERCHANT NO. 1:   Of something grand!

ALL: Something awesome, something wondrous
                    Will take place in Bethlehem,
                    Will take place in Bethlehem!

                    (Verse 1)
SILAS: Can't explain it!

MERCHANT NO. 2:   Can't contain it!

ALL: So much is still a myst'ry.

SILAS: Can't ignore it!

TOWNSPERSON NO. 1: Must explore it!

ALL: Tonight we're changing hist'ry!

SILAS: Something big's about to happen
                    Right here in Bethlehem!

                    (Chorus)
SILAS: It's in our hearts!

TOWNSPERSON NO. 1: It's on the wind!

ALL: Something good is waiting around the bend!

TOWNSPERSON NO. 2: We're on the brink

MERCHANT NO. 1:   Of something grand!

ALL: Something awesome, something wondrous
                    Will take place in Bethlehem,
                    Will take place in Bethlehem!

                    (Verse 2)
MERCHANT NO. 2:   Don't debate it!
                    Can't negate it!

ALL: Get set for celebration!

MERCHANT NO. 1:   Don't know why yet!
                    Can't deny it!

ALL: It's time for jubilation!

SILAS: Something big's about to happen
                    Right here in Bethlehem!

	(Chorus)
SILAS:	It's in our hearts!

TOWNSPERSON NO. 1: It's on the wind!

ALL: Something good is waiting around the bend!

TOWNSPERSON NO. 2: We're on the brink

MERCHANT NO. 1: Of something grand!

ALL: Something awesome, something wondrous
Will take place in Bethlehem,
Will take place in Bethlehem!

(The following is spoken.)

MERCHANT NO. 2: Next week?

SILAS: No. It's much more imminent than that.

TOWNSPERSON NO. 1: Tomorrow?

SILAS: No, not tomorrow.

TOWNSPERSON NO. 2: We're on the brink . . .

MERCHANT NO. 1: Of something marvelous . . .

MERCHANT NO. 2: Something astounding . . .

TOWNSPERSON NO. 1: Even miraculous!

ALL *(sung):* Something awesome, something wondrous
Will take place in Bethlehem,
Will take place in Bethlehem . . .

SILAS *(spoken or shouted or sung by all):* Tonight!

(TOWNSPEOPLE *and* MERCHANTS *resume their activities.)*

BARTHOLOMEW *(to* SILAS): You know, I feel it too. It's as though the voice of an angel is riding on the wind, gently stirring us to action.

MARTHA *(from offstage):* Bartholomew! Get to work!

BARTHOLOMEW: That wasn't it.

(BARTHOLOMEW *and* SILAS *get back to work.)*

(Blackout)

Scene 7

Characters: MARY
JOSEPH
SILAS
MARTHA
LEAH (BARTHOLOMEW *and* MARTHA's *daughter, about 10 or 12 years of age)*

Setting: Streets of Bethlehem, with both motels

Props: No Vacancy sign

Costumes: Bible-time clothes

(As the lights come up, we see MARY *and* JOSEPH *making their way through the streets of Bethlehem. They approach the Motel Six Shekels, but just as* JOSEPH *is about to rap on the door,* SILAS *comes out and hangs up the No Vacancy sign.)*

SILAS *(seeing* MARY *and* JOSEPH*):* Sorry.

*(*SILAS *goes back into his motel.* JOSEPH *and* MARY *make their way over to the Bethlehem Inn.* JOSEPH *knocks on the door.* MARTHA *opens it.)*

MARTHA: Can I help you?

JOSEPH: We'd like a room for the night.

MARTHA: I never thought I'd live to say this, but we're completely booked for the night. I told my husband to hang up the No Vacancy sign, but you think he'd do it? The man is going to drive me to *(noticing* MARY*)* . . . well, I see you've got your own worries. I wish I could help. Have you tried the other inns?

JOSEPH: We've tried them all. You were our last hope.

MARTHA: Sorry. There's nothing I can do.

LEAH *(appears in doorway):* They can have my room, Mother.

MARTHA: Your room indeed, young lady. You'd do anything to get to stay up late with the adults. Now, off to bed.

LEAH: But, Mother, you can't turn them away. Who knows who that baby's going to grow up to be someday.

MARTHA: Even if he were a king, we still have no room. (*To* MARY *and* JOSEPH) Sorry.

(MARTHA *shuts the door.* MARY *and* JOSEPH *turn and start walking away. After a few seconds,* LEAH *opens the window and calls to them.*)

LEAH: Wait! I have an idea. Don't leave . . .

(MARY *and* JOSEPH *wait, as* LEAH *disappears into her home. After a few seconds, both* MARTHA *and* LEAH *appear in the doorway.*)

MARTHA (*hesitantly*): My daughter seems to think that you might be willing to stay in our . . . well, in (LEAH *pulls at her skirt, as if coaxing her to say it.*) She thinks you might want to stay in our stable . . . Kids—you just never know what they're going to say.

JOSEPH: We'd be happy to stay there.

MARTHA (*to* LEAH): See, I told you I shouldn't even bother . . . (*She realizes what* JOSEPH *just said.*) What'd you say?

JOSEPH: As you can see, my wife's time is almost here. We'd be happy with shelter of *any* kind.

MARTHA: I suppose the stables are better than nothing. Come. It's just a short walk.

(MARTHA *leads* MARY *and* JOSEPH *offstage. After they exit,* LEAH *sings "When You Make Room for Him."*)

When You Make Room for Him

(*Verse 1*)
LEAH: Don't turn away.
    It's time to say
    "Come in."
    Don't let Him go.
    You need to know
    This friend.
    He won't impose
    But gently shows
    The way.
    Oh, why not begin
    New life in Him
    Today?

(*Chorus*)
When you make room for Him,
There's no room left for fears.
It's too crowded for doubting,

And it's too full for tears.
When you make room for Him,
There's no room for despair.
You'll find joy everlasting,
And peace in His care,
When you make room for Him.

(Verse 2)
Never assume
You don't have room
For Him.
Don't turn your back,
You'll never lack
Again.
You have a choice,
Lift up your voice
And say:
Oh, I want a new start,
Come in my heart
Today.

(Chorus)
When you make room for Him,
There's no room left for fears.
It's too crowded for doubting,
And it's too full for tears.
When you make room for Him,
There's no room for despair.
You'll find joy everlasting,
And peace in His care,
When you make room for Him.
    You'll find joy everlasting
    and peace in His care,
    When you make room, room for Him.

(Blackout)

Scene 8

Characters: SHAMICH
JOSIAH
HEBOAM
TYRUS

Setting: A field outside Bethlehem

Props: Shepherds' staffs
A pot of stew
Bowls
Eating utensils

Costumes: Shepherd-wear

(Scene opens with the shepherds sitting in the field, eating their stew and talking. The pot of stew is off to the side.)

SHAMICH: Is it just me, or do the stars seem brighter tonight?

JOSIAH: There does seem to be more light . . . unfortunately.

SHAMICH: Unfortunately?

JOSIAH: Now we can see what all you've been putting in this stew!

HEBOAM: It tasted better when it was a mystery!

SHAMICH *(stirring the pot of stew):* Those wishing to complain about the food should be advised—the cook's job stands open. *(He holds out the spoon.)* Any takers? *(There aren't any.)* I didn't think so. *(He scoops himself another bowl. Looks at it, grimaces, then when others aren't looking, he scrapes it back into the pot.)*

HEBOAM *(a beat):* So, whose night is it to keep watch?

JOSIAH: I had last night.

SHAMICH: And I the night before.

TYRUS: Why don't we *all* get some sleep? After all, what could happen in one night?

JOSIAH: Are you serious? *Everything* could happen.

37

SHAMICH: Besides, we're the shepherds. We can't just leave our flock unattended all night long.

HEBOAM: You know, my brothers, I've had a feeling all day that something big was going to happen tonight.

TYRUS: You're just trying to get me to stay awake.

HEBOAM: No. I can't explain it. But somehow tonight is special . . . to us . . . to Bethlehem . . . maybe even to the whole world.

TYRUS: That's the stew talking.

SHAMICH: I understand what Heboam is saying. I've been feeling it too.

TYRUS: All right, all right. I'll keep watch. But if tonight passes and not a single thing happens, I'm not going to believe any of you next time.

(The other shepherds lay down and start dozing off, as TYRUS *keeps watch.)*

(Blackout)

Scene 9

Characters:	MARY JOSEPH BABY JESUS
Setting:	Stable
Props:	Manger Hay Various items to give the look of a stable
Costumes:	Bible-time clothes Swaddling clothes for Baby Jesus
Sound Effect:	Baby crying

(It is night. MARY *has just delivered* BABY JESUS. *We hear the sound effects of a baby crying.)*

JOSEPH *(handing the* BABY JESUS *to* MARY): Mary, look. He's beautiful.

MARY: He is, isn't He?

JOSEPH: It's hard to believe that the Messiah would be born here . . . in a stable.

MARY: His royalty doesn't come from where He was born but from who He is. *(To* BABY JESUS) Jesus . . . holy Son of God, welcome to Your world.

(MARY *sings "Jesus, Welcome to Your World" after she places* BABY JESUS *in the manger.)*

Jesus, Welcome to Your World
(two other female voices are optional)

(Verse 1)
MARY: You left Your Father's side to come here,
Left a throne for one of hay.
Ev'rything that You have sacrificed
is a debt we can't repay.
You left a palace for a stable,
Came from heaven up above.
Messiah sleeping in a manger,
Sent to show the world God's love.

(Chorus)
MARY: Jesus, welcome to Your world.

(OPTIONAL FEMALE VOICES *echo:* Welcome to Your world.)
Is it ev'rything You knew it would be?

MARY *(and* OPTIONAL FEMALE VOICES): Are Your people worth Your love?
Worth the price You'll pay

MARY: at Calvary?

MARY *(or* OPTIONAL FEMALE VOICES): Welcome to Your world.

MARY: I can almost hear the angels sing.

MARY *(and* OPTIONAL FEMALE VOICES): What a precious gift from God.
Bethlehem, behold your newborn king.

MARY *(or* OPTIONAL FEMALE VOICES): Bethlehem, behold your newborn king.

MARY: Jesus, welcome to Your world.

(Verse 2)
MARY: You left the majesty of heaven,
Walked away from streets of gold.
Lamb of God, Your holy birth fulfilled
All the prophecies of old.
You sacrificed Your robe for swaddling clothes,
Took the form of simple man.
Trading in Your crown for one of thorns,
Yielding to God's perfect plan.

(Chorus)
MARY: Jesus, welcome to Your world.

(OPTIONAL FEMALE VOICES *echo:* Welcome to Your world.)
Is it ev'rything You knew it would be?

MARY *(and* OPTIONAL FEMALE VOICES): Are Your people worth Your love?
Worth the price You'll pay

MARY: at Calvary?

OPTIONAL FEMALE VOICES *(or* MARY): Welcome to Your world.

MARY: I can almost hear the angels sing.

MARY *(and* OPTIONAL FEMALE VOICES): What a precious gift from God.
Bethlehem, behold your newborn king.

OPTIONAL FEMALE VOICES *(or* MARY): Bethlehem, behold your newborn king.

MARY: Jesus, welcome to Your world.

OPTIONAL FEMALE VOICES *(or* MARY): Welcome to Your world.

MARY: Welcome to Your world.

OPTIONAL FEMALE VOICES *(or* MARY): Welcome to Your world.

MARY: Jesus, welcome to Your world.

(Blackout)

Scene 10

Characters: SHAMICH
JOSIAH
HEBOAM
TYRUS
ANGEL (Voice over P.A. only)
NARRATOR

Setting: A field outside Bethlehem

Props: Same setting as Scene 8

Costumes: Shepherd-wear for shepherds

(The scene should look the same as scene 8. The shepherds are asleep now, except for TYRUS.)

TYRUS *(to himself):* Nothing's going to happen tonight. Nothing ever happens on my watch. I sit here night after night and not a single thing ever . . .

(A bright, almost blinding light shines on him. As he attempts to shield his eyes, we hear a voice over the P.A. During this, the others begin awakening.)

ANGEL: "Fear not: for, behold, I bring you good tidings of great joy, which shall be to all people. For unto you is born this day in the city of David a Saviour, which is Christ the Lord. And this shall be a sign unto you; Ye shall find the babe wrapped in swaddling clothes, lying in a manger."

(The light shining on the shepherds grows even brighter. TYRUS *awakens others and they look skyward in awe.)*

NARRATOR: "And suddenly there was with the angel a multitude of the heavenly host praising God, and saying, Glory to God in the highest, and on earth peace, good will toward men."

(Blackout)

Finale

Characters: MARY
JOSEPH
BABY JESUS
SHEPHERDS
REST OF CAST

Setting: Stables, then streets of Bethlehem

Props: Manger

Costumes: Bible-time clothing

(Scene opens with MARY *and* JOSEPH *looking down at* BABY JESUS *in the manger. We hear "O Come, All Ye Faithful" (2 verses) sung softly over the P.A. During the song, the shepherds enter, singing along, and gather around Jesus. Then* LEAH, MARTHA, *and* BARTHOLOMEW *join them. On the second verse, the entire cast begins joining the others onstage. They remain on the streets of Bethlehem.* MARTHA, BARTHOLOMEW, *and* LEAH *leave the stable and start spreading the news among the townspeople, who join in singing. After the final chorus of "O Come, All Ye Faithful" the cast sings the finale, which is the final verse and chorus of "Bethlehem's Big Night." During the finale,* MARY, JOSEPH, *and the shepherds continue looking reverently at* BABY JESUS *in the manger.)*

O Come, All Ye Faithful

(Verse 1)
O come, all ye faithful,
joyful and triumphant,
O come ye, O come ye,
to Bethlehem.
Come and behold him,
born the King of angels;

(Chorus)
O come, let us adore him,
O come, let us adore him,
O come, let us adore him,
Christ the Lord.

(Verse 2)
Yea, Lord, we greet Thee,
born this happy morning.
O Jesus, to Thee be all
glory giv'n;
Word of the Father, now in
flesh appearing!

(Chorus)
O come, let us adore him,
O come, let us adore him,
O come, let us adore him,
Christ the Lord.

Bethlehem's Big Night Finale
O Bethlehem, you've made the news!
The word is spreading fast!
Keep basking in the limelight!
You're on the map at last!
O sleepy town, you didn't know
What was to be your fate.
While you were thinking little
God chose to make you great!

(Chorus)
Be-be-be-bethlehem,
Ho-ho-ho-holy town.
What's happened here will clearly
Turn the world right upside down!
The Son of God's been born
Upon this holy morn.
God had some mighty big plans
For you, O Bethlehem!
God had some mighty big plans
For you, O Bethlehem!

BARTHOLOMEW *(spoken):* You may be small, but . . .

CAST *(sings):*
God had some mighty *big* plans
For you, O Bethlehem!

(Blackout)

❄

ADDITIONAL YULETIDE SKETCHES

The Scrooge Patrol

Characters: OFFICER WILLIAMS
GLADYS NEWBAUM

Setting: Department store

Props: Various props indicating that we are in a department store
Police report book

Costumes: Security uniform for Officer Williams
Modern-day wear for Gladys Newbaum

(Sketch opens with GLADYS *shopping.* OFFICER WILLIAMS *approaches her.)*

OFFICER: Excuse me, miss, but I'm afraid you'll have to come with me.

GLADYS: What seems to be the problem, Officer?

OFFICER *(taking her arm):* Just come with me, and there won't be any trouble.

GLADYS: But . . .

OFFICER: I've had my eye on you ever since you walked into this store.

GLADYS: But I haven't broken any laws.

OFFICER: Our security cameras got it all on videotape.

GLADYS: Got *what* all on videotape?

OFFICER: Don't play innocent with me. We've been busy building quite a case against you. *(He lets go of her arm and opens his report book.)*

GLADYS: A case?

OFFICER *(reading from report book):* We caught you red-handed on aisle 14.

GLADYS: Doing what?

OFFICER: Being polite to another customer. That's a direct violation of the Christmas Shopper's Code of Conduct.

GLADYS: Christmas Shopper's Code of Conduct? I didn't even know there was such a thing.

47

OFFICER: Ignorance of the law is no excuse.

GLADYS: OK, so I was polite. That's still not enough to book me on.

OFFICER: Did I say I was done? We also witnessed what you did on aisle 12.

GLADYS: And exactly what was that?

OFFICER: You don't remember? How convenient. Well, let me refresh your memory. When the lady rolled her stroller over your foot, all you did was smile and wish her happy holidays.

GLADYS: What's wrong with that?

OFFICER: You were clearly exceeding the Christmas cheer limit. . . . And we were watching you out in the parking lot too.

GLADYS: What'd I do wrong out there?

OFFICER: You saw an empty space the same time as another driver.

GLADYS: Yeah . . . so?

OFFICER: You didn't fender fight him over it. You just backed up and let him take it.

GLADYS: It seemed like the right thing to do. I knew I'd find another one in an hour or two.

OFFICER: Look . . . Christmas shoppers have worked years to perfect their impatient and "me first" image. You can't just come along and erase all that with a few pleases and thank yous. This is Christmas . . . what does kindness and consideration have to do with it?

GLADYS: Officer, Christmas is *all* about kindness and consideration . . . and love. You see, it's like this: I figure if God could demonstrate His love to the world by sending His Son some 2,000 years ago, the least I can do is help spread a little of that love around too.

OFFICER: But you're setting a precedent here. Do you have any idea what could happen if everyone acted like you at Christmas?

GLADYS: You'd be out of a job?

OFFICER: Exactly.

GLADYS: Imagine it—everyone treating each other with manners and consideration. That'd be a pretty nice way to celebrate the Lord's birthday, wouldn't it?

OFFICER (*thinks for a moment*): Manners and consideration instead of pushing and shoving? It'll never catch on.

GLADYS: We've got to start somewhere.

OFFICER *(thinks for a moment):* Well, I *have* been wanting to take some time off. And it sure would save me a lot of paperwork.

GLADYS: So, are you dropping the charges?

OFFICER *(a beat):* I suppose I could release you . . . for good behavior.

GLADYS: Good behavior . . . now that's something I don't mind being accused of. Merry Christmas, Officer.

OFFICER: Merry Christmas!

(Blackout)

THE SWEATSHOP

Characters: ANNETTE
FRANCINE

Setting: Presumably at one of their homes

Props: Two chairs
Two basins
Kettle, with water
Two towels

Costumes: Sweats
Sweatbands

(Sketch opens with ANNETTE *and* FRANCINE *sitting on the chairs, soaking their feet in the basins. Their sweat pants are rolled up to their knees, and they each have a towel around their neck. The kettle is next to them, presumably filled with hot water.)*

ANNETTE *(moaning and wiping her brow with the towel):* Ohhhhhhhhh . . . What a workout!

FRANCINE: Every muscle in my body aches.

ANNETTE: I told you we shouldn't have done the advanced routine. Start simple . . . that's what I said. But would you listen? Noooooo.

FRANCINE: So, how many pounds do you figure we lifted today?

ANNETTE: Let's see . . . five packages per arm, with wrapping and bows . . . I'd say a hundred pounds easy!

FRANCINE: I can feel my biceps pumping even as we speak.

ANNETTE: You mean, even as we gasp. I still haven't caught my breath.

FRANCINE: It was all that sprinting we did from store to store that really wore me out.

ANNETTE: Yeah . . . who would have thought Christmas shopping would be such strenuous exercise?

FRANCINE *(rubbing her knees):* I think I pulled a muscle when I leaped over that counter.

ANNETTE: You had no choice. It was the quickest way to get to the sale bin. *(Lifting kettle)* More hot water?

FRANCINE: Yes, thanks.

(ANNETTE *pours water from the kettle into* FRANCINE'S *basin, then pours some in her own. For safety reasons, it should only be lukewarm.*)

FRANCINE: How many stretches do you think we did?

ANNETTE: I know I did one every time another customer and I would reach for the same blouse.

FRANCINE: Well, I was pretty impressed with your running broad jump.

ANNETTE: How else could I clear all those kids in the toy department? . . . And, say, I didn't know you could bend over and touch your toes like that.

FRANCINE: My high heel got caught in the escalator. It was the only way I could get it loose.

ANNETTE: All I know is I haven't gotten this much exercise since my Jane Fonda tape accidentally kicked into fast forward during one of my workouts.

FRANCINE: We probably wouldn't be so sore if we had done our warm-up exercise first.

ANNETTE: What do you call that four-mile jog we did from our parking space to the mall entrance?

FRANCINE: That's right. I forgot all about that.

ANNETTE: How could you forget? They had to send a rescue team out twice to look for us.

FRANCINE: What really got my heart to pumping was the workout we got at the checkout counter.

ANNETTE: All that running in place?

FRANCINE: No. Signing all those charge slips. My heart hasn't beat that fast in years.

ANNETTE: We must have burned off 3,000 calories!

FRANCINE: So, what'dya say? Are we on for tomorrow?

ANNETTE: Same time, same mall?

FRANCINE *(they nod confidentially and shake hands):* And who says the holidays are bad for your figure?

(They both sit back and ooh and ahhh as they pour more water into their basins.)

(Blackout)

TREE TALK

Characters: ANGEL TREETOP
TOY SOLDIER ORNAMENT
CANDY CANE
BALL ORNAMENT

Setting: The top of a Christmas tree (The set should look like the upper portion of the tree only.)

Props: Tinsel garland
Christmas tree decorations

Costumes: Angel costume
Soldier costume
Candy cane costume
Ball ornament costume

Sound Effects: Music box style Christmas music

(Sketch opens with the angel standing at the highest point of the tree. Our other three characters are near her, as if hanging from a lower branch.)

BALL ORNAMENT *(looking downward):* Look at them down there . . . ripping open their presents faster than you can say, "No payments till February." Don't they know what this day is really all about?

ANGEL TREETOP: Yeah . . . I'm not up here for my health. I'm petrified of heights! I stand here year after year two inches from the ceiling with a tree branch scratching my back for one reason and one reason only—to remind people that Christmas can be summed up in four simple words.

TOY SOLDIER ORNAMENT: That's *my* parking space?

ANGEL TREETOP: No. "For God so loved."

CANDY CANE: That's right. Today is the anniversary of the day when God gave His only begotten Son to the world.

BALL ORNAMENT: I know that, and you know that, but sometimes people get so busy celebrating the holiday, they forget who the celebration is for.

(We hear some music box type Christmas music beginning to play.)

TOY SOLDIER ORNAMENT: Ut-oh.

ANGEL TREETOP: What's the matter?

TOY SOLDIER ORNAMENT: My music's starting.

CANDY CANE: So?

TOY SOLDIER ORNAMENT: Whenever my music starts, something very embarrassing happens.

BALL ORNAMENT: Like what?

TOY SOLDIER ORNAMENT: Like this. (*As if completely beyond his control, he does a goofy little wooden soldier march and turn.*) Oh, why'd I have to be one of those mechanical ornaments? (*He makes one last turn.*) . . . Catch you on the way back.

(*The music stops, and the soldier stops his march.*)

ANGEL TREETOP: That wasn't so bad.

TOY SOLDIER ORNAMENT: You do it 385 times a day and see how much fun it is!

CANDY CANE: Well, at least you've got something to do. All I do is just hang here and draw flies.

(*They almost lose their balance, as though someone just shook the tree.*)

TOY SOLDIER ORNAMENT (*to someone apparently at the bottom of the tree*): Hey, watch it, kid! (*To others*) He got so excited grabbing his gifts, he almost knocked the whole tree over!

ANGEL TREETOP (*straightening herself*): He didn't even look up here to see if we're all right.

BALL ORNAMENT: They don't care. I almost got knocked out by a flying wad of tissue paper four presents ago. I'm used to it.

CANDY CANE: It's good that they exchange gifts, and I can live with them ignoring us, but how can they go on ignoring the One who's at the very heart of Christmas?

ANGEL TREETOP: Wait a minute . . . maybe they're not ignoring us. Listen . . . do you hear that?

CANDY CANE: Hear what?

ANGEL TREETOP: That music.

TOY SOLDIER ORNAMENT: Oh, no . . . not again already. (*He prepares for his little march and turn.*)

ANGEL TREETOP: It's not *your* music. This sounds like Christmas carols. They're singing *Christmas carols!*

CANDY CANE: Are you sure it's not the MasterCard jingle?

BALL ORNAMENT: No, it's Christmas carols. Real people singing real Christmas carols.

CANDY CANE *(pointing):* And look . . . one of them's opening a Bible, and they're beginning to read the Christmas story.

TOY SOLDIER ORNAMENT: Are we in the right house?

BALL ORNAMENT *(looking around):* This is the right house, but I still say we check everyone's I.D.

ANGEL TREETOP: No . . . they're our family, all right. But I've never seen them act like this!

CANDY CANE: I wonder what's come over them?

TOY SOLDIER ORNAMENT: Yeah . . . don't they know there are more gifts under the tree?

BALL ORNAMENT: Maybe they finally remembered whose birthday it is.

ANGEL TREETOP: And look . . . they're even pointing up here to me. They must be at the part where the angel tells the good news of Jesus' birth.

TOY SOLDIER ORNAMENT: You know, it's moments like this that make waiting in our box all year long worth it.

CANDY CANE: I agree.

BALL ORNAMENT: Merry Christmas

OTHERS: Merry Christmas

(Music box music starts again.)

TOY SOLDIER ORNAMENT: Ut-oh . . . here we go again. *(He starts doing his march and turn.)* And with my luck, they stuck those batteries in me that keep going . . . and going . . . and going . . .

(He continues marching and turning, as the others shrug their shoulders.)

(Blackout)

SHOPPER STOPPER

Character: ANNOUNCER

Props: A small patch (like a Dramamine patch)
A giant patch (same shape as above, but about a foot bigger. This should be folded.)

(ANNOUNCER *stands center stage. Both patches are in his pocket.*)

ANNOUNCER: Are your spending habits out of control? No matter how many times you've tried to quit, do you still find yourself reaching for that one last purchase? The one final sale?

You've tried everything—weekend clinics, seminars, chewing gum, but nothing is powerful enough to get rid of that overwhelming desire to "shop till you drop"? Even the warning on your credit cards that reads "Overuse of this product can be hazardous to your wealth," isn't enough to deter you from trying to purchase the entire sportswear department at Macy's.

And now with the holidays upon us, you're afraid you're not going to be able to stand up to the temptation of all the "Pre-Christmas sales," "Christmas Eve markdowns," and "After Christmas clearances." After all, you *are* only human.

Well, my friend, don't dismay because I'm here to tell you there's hope!

You've heard of "motion sickness patches" and "Nicotine patches"? Well, now there's the "Shopper's patch." Simply place it behind your ear like this *(he demonstrates)*, and it'll get those shopping urges back under control. With the Shopper's Patch, you'll be able to drive away from a mall without having to rent a trailer bed for your purchases. You'll be able to let a store manager lock up at closing time without calling Security to pry your fingers from the door. Your creditors will be able to deliver those February deferred billing statements to your house by parcel post, instead of by crane.

And for you more serious shoppers, try the Super Size Shopper's Patch. *(He takes the jumbo Shopper's Patch from his pocket and unfolds it.)* Whatever your needs, we have a Shopper's Patch sized just for you.

So remember—the Shopper's Patch; don't enter a mall without it!

(Blackout)

I DID IT ALL MYSELF

Characters: Director (may be played by male or female)
Phil (if played by female—Phyllis)
Don
Lucy

Setting: Christmas pageant stage

Props: None needed

Costumes: Modern-day wear

Sound Effect: Set crashing

(Sketch opens with a frazzled Director *talking with* Phil *on the Christmas pageant stage.)*

Director: If I even think about volunteering to direct a Christmas pageant again, I give you full permission to tie me up in tinsel and tape my mouth shut!

Phil: Things aren't going well?

Director *(sarcastically):* Oh, they're going wonderfully! First of all, none of our costumes turned out right.

Phil: That happens sometimes. No matter how hard you try, they can still end up too tight or too loose on the actors.

Director: Our costume designer forgot the holes for their heads to go through! And you wouldn't believe all the trouble we've been having with the sets. At our last rehearsal, one of the flats fell over during our shepherd scene. It was that one over there, with Bethlehem painted on it. *(He points to an imaginary flat.)* The shepherd's line was, "We're almost there. I can see Bethlehem getting closer and closer." Those poor shepherds had no idea just how close Bethlehem really was getting. The next thing they knew, it hit them on the head!

Phil: Sounds like you need to assemble a better crew next time.

Director: Crew? I did it all myself. I couldn't trust such important jobs as the costumes and sets to just anyone. And you should have seen the spotlight at our last rehearsal. It was all over the place.

PHIL: Who was operating it?

DIRECTOR: My five-year-old. He didn't really want to, but I couldn't be in two places at the same time.

PHIL: Why don't you ask some people in the church to help?

DIRECTOR: Oh, no . . . I couldn't do that. I don't want to bother anyone.

PHIL: Bother them? Did it ever occur to you they just might be waiting for an opportunity to use their talents for the Lord?

DIRECTOR: But it's so much work. I can't expect someone to volunteer that kind of time.

(DON *enters.*)

DON *(to* PHIL*):* Excuse me . . . I don't mean to interrupt . . .

PHIL: No, no . . . that's OK. Go right ahead.

DON *(to* DIRECTOR*):* I just wanted you to know that if you need anything for the Christmas pageant, I'd be more than happy to help.

DIRECTOR *(shocked):* Really?

DON: Sure. I'm a finish carpenter, and I also have some art background. I'd love to be involved—you know, making sets or whatever.

DIRECTOR: That's great. Our rehearsals are Monday nights. Can you come out this Monday so we can talk about it?

DON: I'll be there.

(DON *exits.*)

PHIL: See, and you thought . . .

(LUCY *enters.*)

LUCY *(to* PHIL*):* My husband's waiting out in the car. Can I interrupt you for just a second?

PHIL: Of course.

LUCY *(to* DIRECTOR*):* I just wanted you to know that if you need any help on the costumes for the play, I've been a seamstress for 18 years.

DIRECTOR: Well, a few of our costumes could use some work.

LUCY: Just give me a call. *(Turns to leave, then)* You know, I can't sing in the choir or play a musical instrument for the Lord, but I can sew. I like to think of it as my ministry. *(We hear a car horn offstage.)* . . . That's my husband. Gotta go.

DIRECTOR: I'll be calling you. And thanks.

(LUCY *smiles and exits.*)

PHIL: And you thought you had to do everything yourself.

DIRECTOR: I didn't realize it, but by trying to carry it all myself, maybe I've been denying others a blessing.

PHIL: God created each of us with different talents. We need to make sure they're being put to use.

DIRECTOR: I see that now. My talent is in directing. Someone else's talent is sewing costumes. And another person's is making sets.

PHIL: Now, you're catching on.

DIRECTOR: But tell me the truth, I didn't do *that* bad of a job on the sets, did I?

PHIL *(looking up):* No . . . they do look pretty nice. . . . But would you mind if we move over a few steps?

DIRECTOR *(as they both move over a couple of steps):* So you can get a better view?

PHIL: No. I think the set's getting ready to go again.

(They both look up, gasp, and take the famous "A wall's getting ready to fall on my head" position.)

DIRECTOR: You know, on second thought, maybe I should meet with that carpenter *this* afternoon!

(They continue ducking, and we . . .

(Blackout)

(Sound effects of a crash)

59

Bethlehem's Big Night

MARTHA BOLTON

BILL WOLAVER
Arr. by Bill Wolaver

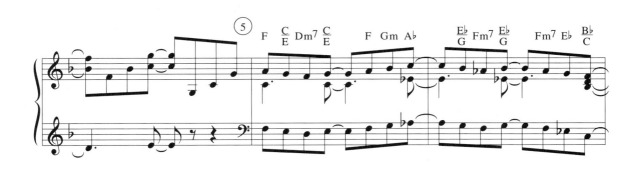

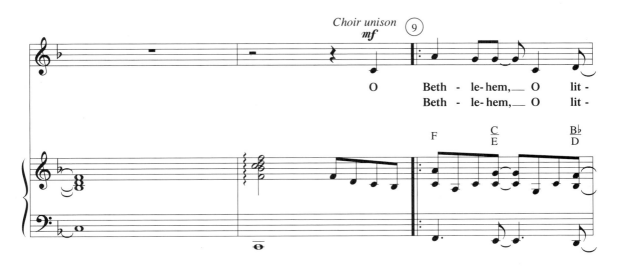

Copyright © 1995 by Pilot Point Music. All rights reserved.
Administered by The Copyright Company, 40 Music Square East, Nashville, TN 37203.

You're Welcome Here

Martha and Ruth

MARTHA BOLTON

BILL WOLAVER
Arr. by Bill Wolaver

Copyright © 1995 by Pilot Point Music. All rights reserved.
Administered by The Copyright Company, 40 Music Square East, Nashville, TN 37203.

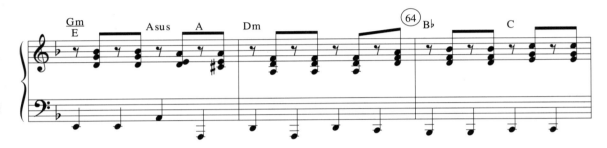

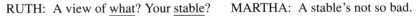

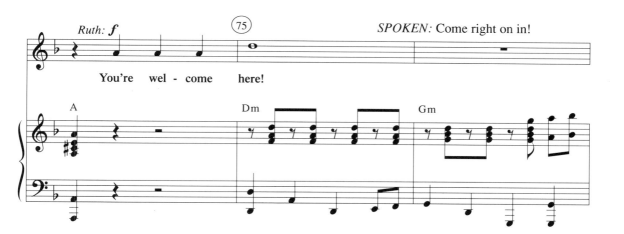
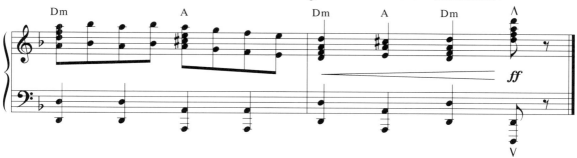

Right Here In Bethlehem

MARTHA BOLTON

BILL and ROBIN WOLAVER
Arr. by Bill Wolaver

TOWNSPERSON 1: *(music begins)* I can't explain it, but it's plainly something great!

TOWNSPERSON 2: Yes, I agree with everything you say!
MERCHANT 1: It's something wonderful!

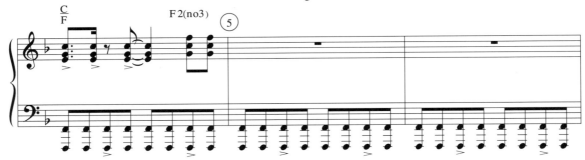

TOWNSPERSON 1: Perhaps stupendous!
SILAS: It just might be the best news to ever come our way!

Copyright © 1995 by Pilot Point Music. All rights reserved.
Administered by The Copyright Company, 40 Music Square East, Nashville, TN 37203.

84

MERCHANT 2: Next week?
SILAS: No. It's much more imminent than that.

TOWNSPERSON 1: Tomorrow?
SILAS: No, not tomorrow.

TOWNSPERSON 2: We're on the brink...
MERCHANT 1: Of something marvelous...

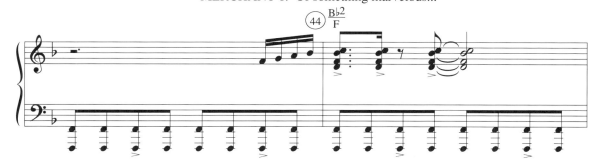

MERCHANT 2: Something astounding...
TOWNSPERSON 1: Even miraculous!

89

When You Make Room for Him
Leah, the Innkeeper's daughter

MARTHA BOLTON

BILL WOLAVER
Arr. by Bill Wolaver

Copyright © 1995 by Pilot Point Music. All rights reserved.
Administered by The Copyright Company, 40 Music Square East, Nashville, TN 37203.

92

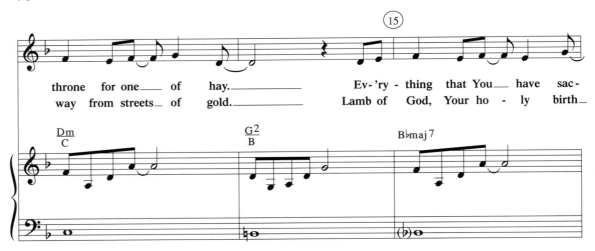
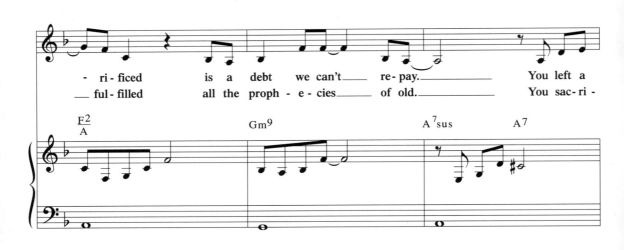

101

Finale

O Come, All Ye Faithful
Bethlehem's Big Night (Reprise)

Arr. by Bill Wolaver

*Arr. © 1995 by Pilot Point Music. All rights reserved. Administered by The Copyright Company, 40 Music Square East, Nashville, TN 37203.

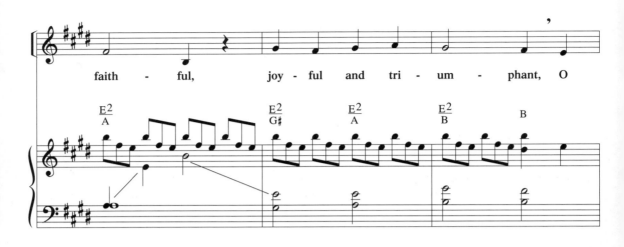

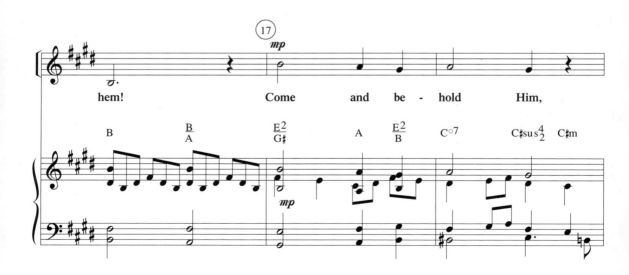

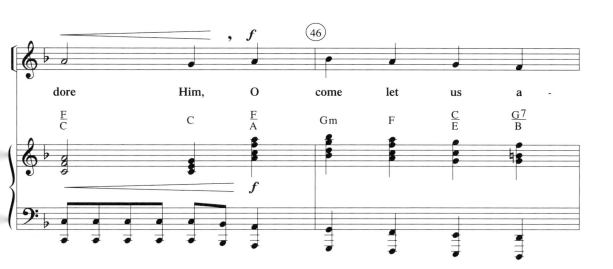

106

*"Bethlehem's Big Night" (Wolaver)

*Copyright © 1995 by Pilot Point Music. All rights reserved. Administered by The Copyright Company, 40 Music Square East, Nashville, TN 37203.

PERFORMANCE LICENSING AGREEMENT

Lillenas Drama Resources
Performance Licensing
P.O. Box 419527, Kansas City, MO 64141

Name _____

Organization _____

Address _____

City _____ State _____ ZIP _____

Play _____

Number of performances intended _____

Approximate dates _____

Amount remitted* $_____

Mail to Lillenas at the address above

Order performance copies of this script from your local bookstore or directly from the publisher.

*$15.00 for the first performance; $10.00 each subsequent performance

PERFORMANCE LICENSING AGREEMENT

**Lillenas Drama Resources
Performance Licensing
P.O. Box 419527, Kansas City, MO 64141**

Name _____

Organization _____

Address _____

City _____ State _____ ZIP _____

Play _____

Number of performances intended _____

Approximate dates _____

Amount remitted* $ _____

Mail to Lillenas at the address above

Order performance copies of this script from your local bookstore or directly from the publisher.

*$15.00 for the first performance; $10.00 each subsequent performance